IMAGES
of America

THE COAST GUARD
IN HAMPTON ROADS

U. S. COAST GUARD

A SYMBOL of SERVICE

"Semper Paratus"

**Under this Flag you may render a great
service in the protection of life and
property on land or sea.**

·ENLIST·

The United States has relied on Hampton Roads, Virginia, during every major conflict over the past 230-plus years. This is certainly true for the US Coast Guard. In this 1930s poster that could be found all over Hampton Roads, the Coast Guard put out the call for young men and women to join and "render a great service in the protection of life and property on land or sea." (Courtesy of the US Coast Guard.)

ON THE COVER: This 1943 photograph from the Office of War Information shows a Coast Guard officer on a pier in Norfolk escorted by armed Coast Guardsmen in "blitz buggies" as he inspects the vigilant waterfront patrols that guarded vital war supplies being shipped across the Atlantic. An official order of the day from Vice Adm. Russell R. Waesche, commandant of the US Coast Guard, read "Vital war shipping must be protected on the docks . . . as well as on the high seas." (Courtesy of the National Archives.)

IMAGES
of America

THE COAST GUARD
IN HAMPTON ROADS

LT Christopher G. Miller, USN (Retired)

ARCADIA
PUBLISHING

Published by Arcadia Publishing
Charleston, South Carolina

Printed in the United States of America

Library of Congress Control Number: 2021948610

For all general information, please contact Arcadia Publishing:
Telephone 843-853-2070
Fax 843-853-0044
E-mail sales@arcadiapublishing.com
For customer service and orders:
Toll-Free 1-888-313-2665

Visit us on the Internet at www.arcadiapublishing.com

To the Coast Guard men and women, past and present, who have devoted their lives to the core values of Honor, Respect, and Devotion to Duty. Semper Paratus!

CONTENTS

ACKNOWLEDGMENTS

This book could not have been possible without the help of Dr. Bill Thiesen, Coast Guard historian for the US Coast Guard (USCG) Atlantic Area, the Mariner's Museum in Newport News, the Sargeant Memorial Collection of the Norfolk Public Library, the special collections of the Portsmouth Public Library, and the Library of Virginia. I would also like to thank my Coast Guard family at Education and Training Quota Management Command. Finally, I would like to thank my husband, James, for his unwavering support.

INTRODUCTION

Hampton Roads is located within the Coast Guard's District 5. It is perhaps the most historic district within the Coast Guard, having witnessed the service's founding, much of its early history, and certainly its future.

Coast Guard men, women, and assets associated with the area began playing a vital role in Coast Guard history the year the Constitution was signed. An act passed by Congress in Philadelphia in 1789 established the US Lighthouse Service, a predecessor agency of the modern Coast Guard. Many US Lighthouse Service firsts were recorded in Hampton Roads, including the first lighthouse built for the federal government at Cape Henry, Virginia, in 1793; the first lightship in service history near Norfolk, Virginia, in 1820; and the tallest lighthouse in the United States, erected at Cape Hatteras in 1870.

In Philadelphia, Congress passed Alexander Hamilton's plan to establish a fleet of revenue cutters, which was the basis for the Revenue Cutter Service. One of the original 10 cutters was based in Hampton Roads—*Virginia* (Norfolk).

Not surprisingly, Coast Guard personnel and assets from the Hampton Roads region have served in every major military conflict. In 1798, four revenue cutters that fought in the Quasi-War with France were built or homeported in the region. During the War of 1812, various cutters in the District 5 region battled warships of the Royal Navy. In June 1812, Norfolk US Revenue Cutter (USRC) *Thomas Jefferson* made the first capture of the war: British schooner *Patriot* bound to Halifax with a cargo of sugar. In 1813, some of the first Coast Guard POWs were captured off the cutter *Surveyor* at the Battle of Gloucester Point near the York River. Revenue cutter captain Samuel Travis was released on parole by the British and returned to his home in Williamsburg, but the enlisted crew was imprisoned at Halifax.

The nation's first and only presidential command vessel, USRC *Miami*, steamed under Pres. Abraham Lincoln in 1861 when he oversaw the amphibious landing of Union troops that re-captured Norfolk. In 1861, Revenue Cutter Service gunboat *Naugatuck* engaged the Confederate ironclad CSS *Virginia* in Hampton Roads shortly before the famous ironclad was scuttled and burned by its crew in the James River.

In 1848, Congress passed legislation that led to the establishment of the US Life-Saving Service. The first lifesaving stations were placed along the New Jersey shore in the late 1840s. Later, the lifesaving service oversaw one for the Chesapeake Bay and Eastern Shore, and one for Southeast Virginia coastlines. Many notable families have been associated with lifesaving in the District 5 region, including the Burruses, Balances, Grays, O'Neals, and Danielses, while others have cutter namesake members such as Bailey Barco, Benjamin Dailey, Richard Etheridge, and John Midgett.

Women and minorities from the Hampton Roads region blazed a trail in US history while serving in Coast Guard predecessor services. Beginning in the 1820s, women began serving as lighthouse keepers around the Chesapeake Bay. They were the first women in US history to oversee a federal installation. In 1858, USRC *Harriet Lane* became the first cutter to bear a woman's name.

Its namesake, who hailed from the district's region, was the first lady of the United States when her uncle James Buchanan was president. In 1861, the famed cutter *Harriet Lane* spearheaded the capture of forts guarding the entrance to Hatteras Inlet, North Carolina. After an artillery bombardment from the cutter's guns, Confederate forces coined the term being "harriet laned."

The region had hosted many other minority trailblazers. In the early 1850s, several lightships in Virginia had black caretakers ranging in age from 12 to 14, making them the youngest overseers of federal vessels in American history. After the Civil War, African Americans were appointed as lighthouse keepers on the Chesapeake Bay. For example, keeper Richard Etheridge was the officer-in-charge at the Pea Island Lifesaving Station. They were the first minorities in US history to oversee federal installations. Surfman Jeremiah Munden died in 1876 when the Jones Hill (North Carolina) Lifesaving Station crew was lost in a rescue attempt. He was the first African American surfman to die in the line of duty.

After the formation of the modern Coast Guard, Hampton Road's minorities continued to break barriers. In 1938, Chippewa Tribe member and chief radioman Howard Kischassey took charge of the Coast Guard radio station at Dam Neck, Virginia, becoming the first Native American officer-in-charge of a station in the service. In 1922, African American boatswain George Pruden advanced to chief petty officer and took charge of the Pea Island Lifesaving Station that same year. In 1915, just before US entry into World War I, the Life-Saving Service and Revenue Cutter Service merged to form the Coast Guard. The new service adopted a hybrid of the lifesaving service system with the forerunner of District 5, the Norfolk Division, encompassing much of the territory currently overseen by District 5. During World War I, Coast Guard bases, installations, and assets in District 5 kept watch day and night. In 1918, the service lost the *Diamond Shoal* lightship to U-boat attack off the North Carolina coast.

During World War II, the Coast Guard was transferred from the Treasury Department to the Navy, and it adopted the Navy's district system, which it has retained ever since. During the war, cutters battled Nazi submarines in an area off the North Carolina coast called "Torpedo Junction." Chincoteague, Virginia, native and mustang officer Maurice Jester commanded the cutter *Icarus* in the sinking of *U-352* off the coast of North Carolina. This historic event resulted in the war's second U-boat sinking by US forces, the first US capture of enemy combatants, and a Navy Cross medal awarded to Jester. In addition, the fast response cutter (FRC) *Daniel Tarr* bears the name of the Chincoteague hero and Silver Star Medal recipient who operated a landing craft at Guadalcanal.

Coast Guard men and women in Hampton Roads have had to defend the coast against two foes: wartime enemies and Mother Nature. In 1806, North Carolina cuttermen lost their lives in the line of duty when revenue cutters *Diligence III* and *Governor Williams* were destroyed by a super-hurricane at Ocracoke, North Carolina. One hundred and forty years later, during World War II, Coast Guard cutters *Jackson* and *Bedloe* were caught in the open when the Great Atlantic Hurricane swept the North Carolina coast. Both cutters were capsized by rogue waves near the eye of the storm, killing over half of their intrepid crewmembers. In 2018, Hurricane Florence devastated eastern North Carolina, serving as a reminder—like other local hurricanes such as Fran, Floyd, Isabel, Sandy, and Matthew—that Coast Guard men and women often protect the same communities in which they live.

In 1903, worldwide aviation got its start in the area. Interestingly, Coast Guard aviator No. 1 Elmer Stone grew up in Norfolk before attending the Revenue Cutter Service School of Instruction in 1913. While serving on a cutter homeported at Newport News, Virginia, he learned to fly at the Curtis Flying School. He later championed the establishment of a Coast Guard aviation branch. Over 100 years ago, Stone became the first aviator to pilot an aircraft across the Atlantic Ocean when he flew the US Navy's *NC-4* from North America to Europe.

Many other Coast Guard firsts have been recorded in Hampton Roads. In 1906, revenue cutter *Apache* began breaking ice in the Chesapeake Bay. *Apache* was the first cutter fitted out to break ice and tasked with that mission. Also, Capt. Francis Saltus Van Boskerck, composer of the Coast Guard's famous hymn "Semper Paratus," commanded District 5 (then called the Norfolk

District), from 1926 until his death of a heart attack two years later. And many Coast Guard cutter namesakes came from District 5, including World War II heroes Glenn Harris, Oliver Henry, Maurice Jester, and Daniel Tarr; famed commandant Russell Waesche; and Alaska's Revenue Cutter Service hero David Jarvis.

Today, District 5 is headquartered in Portsmouth, Virginia. The Hampton Roads region boasts a large concentration of active duty and retired Coast Guard personnel. It also hosts two headquarter units (Coast Guard and Atlantic Area) and Base Portsmouth.

Indeed, the Coast Guard's history in Hampton Roads is closely tied to District 5. It includes the service's founding, heroes and namesakes, and a legacy of historic firsts. On New Year's Day 1776, the British, having lost control of Portsmouth to the rebels, burned the city to the ground. Recognizing its strategic value and location, a British army soon returned and fortified the area under the command of none other than Benedict Arnold. In the 200 years that have since passed, the value of Portsmouth has not been forgotten. The shared history of Portsmouth and the Coast Guard began in 1820, when the US Lighthouse Service anchored its first lightship off Craney Island. Then the US Lighthouse Service established a lighthouse depot on the Elizabeth River in Portsmouth in 1870 to provide support for aids to navigation in Hampton Roads. In 1939, when the Coast Guard and the Lighthouse Service merged, the depot was expanded and renamed the Portsmouth Coast Guard Base. This base provided support to cutters, aids to navigation, and personnel. As the need emerged, land was purchased to create the only shore-based facility designed by the Coast Guard for the exclusive use of the Coast Guard.

First commissioned as Support Center Portsmouth in 1974, the original 165 military and 130 civilian employees committed to providing quality support products and services to Coast Guard units and personnel throughout the Fifth District area of responsibility. In 1996, a new organization was born: Integrated Support Command (ISC) Portsmouth, whose purpose was to meet the demands of a growing and changing Coast Guard. ISC Portsmouth became the home to six 270s, one 210, one patrol boat, three buoy tenders, and eight other tenant commands, once again providing the superior support customers had come to expect and need. Over the years, the mix and number of cutters and tenant commands have changed, but the mission is the same: to provide excellent mission support to the personnel and assets that call Hampton Roads home. A superb example of this was the support provided after the tragic events of September 11, 2001, when Portsmouth became the processing point for all Coast Guard personnel who volunteered for service.

On November 7, 2009, the Coast Guard honored the city of Portsmouth as a Coast Guard City, one of only eight in the entire country.

This map of Virginia and northern North Carolina has been highlighted to show the Hampton Roads region. The highlight defines the area that Coast Guard Hampton Roads assets patrol. (Courtesy of the US Coast Guard.)

One

LIGHTS

"MIDDLE GROUND LIGHT," SCENE OF ENGAGEMENT BETWEEN THE MERRIMAC AND MONITOR

NORFOLK—NEWPORT NEWS FERRY—THE POPULAR ROUTE   2520-30

This early-20th-century postcard depicts the Norfolk to Newport News ferry and the Middle Ground Light. As described at the top of the card, the area is also famous for being the site of the 1862 Civil War battle between the *Monitor* and the *Merrimack* (CSS *Virginia*). (Courtesy of the Mariner's Museum.)

The Nansemond River Light was located at the confluence of the James and Nansemond Rivers. It was erected in 1878, automated in the 1930s, and completely dismantled in the 1980s. (Courtesy of the National Archives.)

The York Spit Lighthouse was in the York River. It was built in 1853 to replace lightships that previously serviced the area. It was dismantled in the 1960s, and an automated single pole light now stands in its place. (Courtesy of the National Archives.)

Windmill Point Lighthouse was at the entrance to the Rappahannock River. It was built in 1869, repaired in 1921, automated in 1954, and dismantled in 1965. (Courtesy of the National Archives.)

Thimble Shoal Light is a sparkplug lighthouse in the Virginia portion of Chesapeake Bay. This third version of the light was constructed in 1914. The first was built in the 1870s. The two previous lights had been destroyed by natural disasters and wayward ships. It is listed in the National Register of Historic Places. (Courtesy of the National Archives.)

This image shows engineering specs for the Cape Henry shoal light. They were drawn to a .125-inch-to-1-inch scale and were produced in 1905. The plan of the first story shows a kitchen, living room, and bedroom for the lightkeeper. (Courtesy of the National Archives.)

The Wolf Trap Light is a caisson lighthouse at the mouth of Chesapeake Bay. A light has been at this location since 1821. The current lighthouse was built in 1894, automated in 1971, and disestablished in 2017. Today, it is privately owned. (Courtesy of the US Coast Guard.)

This 1893 image shows engineering specs for the foundation pier of the current Wolf Trap Light. This light replaced the previous caisson light that was destroyed by ice in 1893. (Courtesy of the US Coast Guard.)

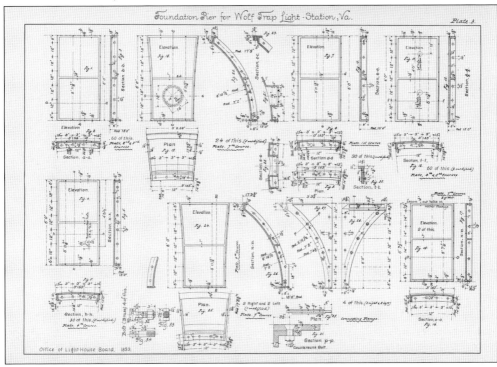

THE BACK RIVER LIGHTHOUSE NEAR FORTRESS MONROE, VA.

This early-20th-century postcard depicts "The Back River Lighthouse near Fortress Monroe, VA." This lighthouse, also known as Grandview Light, was built in 1829, automated in 1915, and destroyed by a hurricane in 1956. (Courtesy of the Mariner's Museum in Newport News).

CH-82— New and Old Lighthouse, Cape Henry, Va. and Marker where First English Colonists Landed

This is an early-20th-century postcard depicting the old and new Cape Henry lighthouses in the background with a cross designating where the first English colonists landed. The site can be visited at First Landing State Park in Virginia Beach. (Courtesy of the US Coast Guard.)

The old Cape Henry Lighthouse is located at Cape Henry, which marks the southern entrance to the Chesapeake in Virginia. The location has long been important for the large amount of ocean-going shipping traffic for the harbors, its rivers, and shipping headed to ports on the bay. The "old" lighthouse was built in 1792, and was the first authorized by the newly formed US government. Visitors can make their way to the top of the lighthouse via a winding staircase for a small fee that supports the maintenance of the structure. (Courtesy of the US Coast Guard.)

The new Cape Henry Lighthouse was built and completed in 1881 after safety concerns over the original light. It and the "old" tower were designated national historic landmarks in 1970. This light is still operational and serves as a critical navigation aid to the heavily trafficked Hampton Roads waterways. (Courtesy of the US Coast Guard.)

This 2012 photograph shows the Assateague Lighthouse on the southeastern shore of Virginia in the Chincoteague National Wildlife Refuge. The light was built in 1867. It is operated and maintained by the US Coast Guard, and it is still used as an aid to navigation. (Courtesy of the National Archives.)

The Smith Point Light is a caisson lighthouse in the Virginia portion of Chesapeake Bay at the mouth of the Potomac River. It was built by the Lighthouse Bureau (a predecessor to the modern Coast Guard) in 1897 and automated in 1971. Lighthouse aficionados may notice its similarity to the Wolf Trap Light, as it was built using the same plans. It was listed in the National Register of Historic Places in 2002. (Courtesy of the National Archives.)

This 1960s image shows crewmembers from the now disestablished USCG Base Norfolk, Berkeley Station, inspecting open ocean buoys. Base Norfolk, sometimes referred to as Berkeley Cutter Base, was disestablished when Base Portsmouth was established. The land is now occupied by commercial shipyards. Norfolk Naval Shipyard is visible in the background. (Courtesy of the Portsmouth Public Library Special Collections.)

This photograph shows a man standing next to a large buoy. The original handwritten caption states that it "towers over the man." Buoys like these can be up to 12 meters in height. (Courtesy of the Portsmouth Public Library Special Collections.)

This is a 1940s-era photograph of an unidentified lightship pier-side in Norfolk. Lightships have a long history, dating back to Roman times. Modern lightships were generally used in locations where a lighthouse or other fixed navigation light was impractical. (Courtesy of the Portsmouth Public Library Special Collections.)

Lightship *Portsmouth* (LV-101) was built in 1915. Her original name was *Charles*, and she served in the Chesapeake Bay outside Cape Charles, Virginia, from 1916 until 1924. The ship was donated to Portsmouth in 1964, moored downtown, and renamed in the city's honor. She was designated a national historic landmark in 1989 and is open to visitors as part of the Portsmouth Naval Shipyard Museum. (Courtesy of the US Coast Guard.)

Chesapeake Light was an offshore lighthouse that marked the entrance to Chesapeake Bay. The structure was first marked with a lightship in the 1930s and was later replaced by a "Texas Tower" in 1965. The lighthouse was eventually automated and was used to support atmospheric measurement for NASA and NOAA. Due to deteriorating structural conditions, the lighthouse was deactivated in 2016 and sold to a private buyer. (Courtesy of the Portsmouth Public Library Special Collections.)

Cape Charles Lighthouse is a tall tower lighthouse at the mouth of the Chesapeake on Smith Island. It was officially removed from service in 2019. It is the tallest lighthouse in Virginia and the second tallest in the United States. (Courtesy of the US Coast Guard.)

This is a recent photograph of the Newport News Middle Ground Light. The light was accepted by the Coast Guard in 1891. It was sold at auction in 2005 to a family from Williamsburg, but it is still an active aid to navigation, and its primary purpose is to designate shoal water in the area. (Courtesy of the National Archives.)

Old Point Comfort Light is located at Fort Monroe in the Virginia portion of Chesapeake Bay. Fort Monroe has long been a strategic asset for the United States. The light was built in 1803. It is the second oldest light in the bay and the oldest still in use. The lighthouse is owned and maintained by the Coast Guard and is listed in the National Register of Historic Places. (Courtesy of the US Coast Guard.)

Cape Henry Station was southeast of Cape Henry Light at what is now Fort Story. It was built in 1874 and deactivated in 1939. The station was demolished by the Army during World War II to clear the ground for defensive shore batteries. (Courtesy of the US Coast Guard.)

The original Little Island Lifesaving Station was constructed in 1878. The site remained an active Coast Guard station until it was inactivated in 1964. The site serves the City of Virginia Beach's Department of Parks and Recreation at Little Island City Park. (Courtesy of the US Coast Guard.)

This early-20th-century photograph shows the Portsmouth Lighthouse Depot. The US Lighthouse Service established a lighthouse depot on the Elizabeth River in Portsmouth in 1870 to provide support for aids to navigation in Hampton Roads, of which there were many. In 1939, when the Coast Guard and the US Lighthouse Service merged, the depot was expanded and renamed the Portsmouth Coast Guard Base. This base provided support to cutters, aids to navigation, and personnel. (Courtesy of the US Coast Guard.)

Two

CUTTERS AND
OTHER VESSELS

The USRC *Gresham* was a cruising cutter and gunboat of the Revenue Cutter Service and US Coast Guard. She was designed specifically for operations on the Great Lakes. However, during World War I, she was transferred to the US Navy. During the war, she patrolled up and down the East Coast. In 1918, *Gresham* saved the crew of the schooner Madrugada after they were hit by a German U-boat off the coast of Virginia. This photograph of her on the Atlantic coast is from around 1900. (Courtesy of the Library of Congress.)

The USCGC *Apache* entered service in 1891 as the USRC *Galveston*. In 1907, she hit the anchored barge *Rowland* in the Chesapeake Bay. She entered service with the US Navy in 1917 during World War I and was assigned to patrol the waters of the Coast Guard Fifth District, including Hampton Roads, during the remainder of the war. This photograph is from around 1900. (Courtesy of the Library of Congress.)

This image shows the gunboat USS *Bancroft* in the Norfolk Naval Shipyard stone drydock, possibly in March 1905, when she was being decommissioned from the navy and turned over to the US Revenue Cutter Service and renamed USRC *Itasca*. (Courtesy of the Library of Congress.)

The USRC *Onondaga* was an Algonquin-class cutter built for service in the Great Lakes. She had a telegraph installed in Norfolk in 1907. She operated at various bases along the East Coast prior to World War I, including significant time in Hampton Roads. She is pictured here in 1901, participating in the America's Cup. (Courtesy of the US Coast Guard.)

This is an April 1936 photograph of Franklin Delano Roosevelt's presidential yacht, the USS *Potomac* (AG-25), at the Norfolk Naval Shipyard in Portsmouth. The president inspected Hampton Roads Naval facilities, visiting Newport News Shipbuilding, Norfolk Naval Shipyard, and Naval Station Norfolk. He also made trips to Fort Monroe and Langley Air Force Base. The USS *Potomac* was launched in 1934 as the USCGC *Electra* (WPC 187), but was converted to serve as a presidential yacht and commissioned into the US Navy in 1936. (Courtesy of the US Coast Guard.)

USCGC *Taney* (WHEC 37) was a high-endurance cutter that served the Coast Guard from 1936 until her decommissioning in 1986. She was the last military vessel on active duty that fought in Pearl Harbor. During the attacks, she was attached to Base Honolulu and was able to assist with harbor defense minutes after the morning attack. From 1972 until her decommissioning, she was stationed in Hampton Roads. In the 1940s photograph above, she is at home in Norfolk. Today, she is a floating museum in Baltimore (below). (Both, courtesy of the US Coast Guard.)

USCGC *Marion* (WSC 145) was an active-class patrol boat that served the Coast Guard from 1927 to 1962. She primarily served out of Norfolk, from 1933 until her decommissioning. She served with the US Navy from 1940 until 1946. She was the first vessel of note to perform oceanographic duties for the Coast Guard. In this early-20th-century photograph, she is at home in Norfolk. (Courtesy of the US Coast Guard.)

The USCGC *Eagle*, a 295-foot tall ship home-ported in New London, Connecticut, is shown transiting the Elizabeth River toward downtown Portsmouth on Friday, September 13, 2013. The *Eagle* is a training ship based at the Coast Guard Academy used primarily to train Coast Guard cadets and officer candidates. (Photograph by PO Brandyn Hill, courtesy of the US Coast Guard.)

The USCGC *Tampa* (WMEC 902) passes near Fort Monroe in Hampton, Virginia. The Hampton Veteran's Affairs hospital can be seen in the distance on the right. USCGC *Tampa* is homeported in Portsmouth. She regularly executes a variety of Coast Guard missions, including drug interdiction, search and rescue, living marine resources, and migrant interdiction. (Courtesy of the US Coast Guard.)

Pre-Commissioning Unit (PCU) *Texas* (SSN 775) sails past the USCGC *Sea Horse* (WPB 87361) in May 2006. The fast-attack submarine returned to the Northrop Grumman Newport News shipyard after successfully completing alpha sea trials to test the boat's capabilities. *Texas* is the second Virginia-class submarine, the first major US Navy combatant vessel class designed with the post–Cold War security environment in mind. (Photograph by Amn. Patrick Gearhiser, courtesy of the US Navy.)

USCGC *Nathan Bruckenthal* (WPC 1128) remains ready at Base Portsmouth in the calm before Hurricane Florence in September 2018. The cutter is full of fuel, sustenance, and her crew, and is standing by to respond and assist post-hurricane. (Photograph by Lt. Bryan Kilcoin, courtesy of the US Coast Guard.)

USCGC *Spencer* (WMEC 905) and USCGC *Escanaba* (WMEC 907) are moored at the pier during a change-of-homeport ceremony at Coast Guard Base Portsmouth on September 8, 2021. The Famous-class cutters are responsible for various Coast Guard missions, including search and rescue, enforcement of laws and treaties, maritime defense, and protection of the environment. (Photograph by PO Paige Hause, courtesy of the US Coast Guard.)

This is a 1933 photograph of the Coast Guard Lake-class cutter *Sebago* docked at Pier 3 at Norfolk Naval Station for the annual Coast Guard cadet cruise in Norfolk. The *Sebago* was launched and commissioned in 1930. After being transferred to the British Royal Navy in 1941 and renamed HMS *Walney*, she was lost in the Allied attack on Oran, Algeria, on November 8, 1942. (Courtesy of the Sergeant Memorial Collection, Norfolk Public Library.)

Cutters from throughout the Fifth Coast Guard District are gathered at Coast Guard Base Portsmouth to participate in a cutter roundup Tuesday, August 22, 2017. The cutter roundup provides joint training opportunities for the crews. (Photograph by Trey Clifton, courtesy of the US Coast Guard.)

Crew members aboard the USCGC *Forward* (WMEC 911) prepare to moor the cutter to the pier at Base Portsmouth, April 27, 2013. The crew aboard the *Forward* patrolled in the Caribbean Sea for 59 days culminating in the rescue of five people, apprehending suspected drug smugglers, and repatriating 75 Haitian migrants. (Photograph by PO Walter Shinn, courtesy of the US Coast Guard.)

A US Coast Guard HH-65A helicopter and a 41-foot utility boat practice helicopter and boat drills in 1996. The HH-65A Dolphin is a short-range recovery helicopter. It is used to perform search and rescue, law enforcement, military readiness, and marine environmental protection missions. The HH-65A can land and take off from 270-foot medium endurance and 378-foot high-endurance cutters. (Courtesy of the US Coast Guard.)

The US Coast Guard Academy flagship *Eagle* sails by the USS *Nassau* (LHA 4) and into Hampton Roads during the opening day of OPSail 2000. Hampton Roads hosted OPSail 2000 and showcased dozens of tall ships from around the world. (Photograph by Amn. Jason Taylor, courtesy of the US Navy.).

The high-endurance cutter USCGC *Chase* (WHEC 718) sits in the floating dry dock *Titan* at the Norfolk Shipbuilding and Drydock Corporation for repairs to its hull in 1991. The guided-missile cruiser USS *Josephus Daniels* (CG 27) is on the other end of the Titan. (Courtesy of the US Coast Guard.)

US Coast Guard vessels and civilian pleasure craft escort the Soviet Sovremenny-class guided-missile destroyer *Otlichnyy* (DDG 434) into Hampton Roads. Officers and crewmen of the *Otlichnyy*, the guided-missile cruiser *Marshal Ustinov* (CG 088), and the replenishment oiler *Genrikh Gasanov* traveled to Naval Station Norfolk for a first-ever five-day goodwill visit in 1989. (Photograph by PO Alan Elliott, courtesy of the US Coast Guard.)

The USCGC *Harriet Lane* (WMEC 903) and USCGC *Northland* (WMEC 904), along with other medium-endurance cutters, are pictured in port at Base Portsmouth in July 1997. (Photograph by PO Telfair Brown, courtesy of the US Coast Guard.)

A helicopter crew from Coast Guard Air Station Elizabeth City conducts a search and rescue demonstration Thursday, October 22, 2015, on the Elizabeth River near Norfolk. The demonstration was part of the 16th annual Towing Vessel Safety Seminar put on by the Coast Guard and the Virginia Maritime Association. (Photograph by PO Trey Clifton, courtesy of the US Coast Guard.)

The USCGC Morro Bay (WTGB 106) conducts ice-breaking operations on the York River. Morro Bay was commissioned March 28, 1981, at the Reserve Training Center in Yorktown and served there until 1998. She is now stationed in New London. This class of ship is primarily stationed in the northeast and on the Great Lakes. They are all named after bays. (Courtesy of the US Coast Guard.)

Two fast-response boats are pictured in Norfolk harbor. These boats can travel at high speed, allowing them to escort high-value assets and pursue bad actors. They are outfitted with crew-served weapons. The Hampton Roads Naval Museum, the USS *Wisconsin*, and a US Navy guided-missile destroyer are in the background. (Courtesy of the US Coast Guard.)

Coast Guard patrol boats escort the aircraft carrier USS *John F. Kennedy* (CV 67) as the vessel approaches the port. *Kennedy* had just returned from deployment in the Persian Gulf area during Operation Desert Storm in 1991. (Courtesy of the National Archives.)

A boy waves a flag as he waits for his father to pull into port at Base Portsmouth onboard the USCGC *Northland* in March 2010. At this homecoming, family members were able to pick out toys courtesy of the Toy Industry Foundation and the Boys and Girls Club. (Photograph by PO Andrew Kendrick, courtesy of the US Coast Guard.)

The USCGC *Legare* (WMEC 912) passes by Pier 9 at Norfolk Naval Base on her way home to Base Portsmouth. The ship returned to port after an emergency underway in preparation for Hurricane Floyd in September 1999. (Courtesy of the US Coast Guard.)

The USCGC *Point Bonita* (WPB 82347) and a Coast Guard 25-foot port security unit Raider boat take part in a hostile party demonstration put on by the Coast Guard for Missions Day attendees. The *Point Bonita* was one of the vessels that participated in Coast Guard Missions Day at Reserve Training Center Yorktown. The purpose of Missions Day is to raise the visibility of the Coast Guard by providing a one-day missions-intensive and hands-on Coast Guard experience to staff-level employees of the federal government. (Photograph by PO Telfair Brown, courtesy of the US Coast Guard.)

The USCGC *Icarus* is pictured in this undated photograph. She is most known for the sinking of German U-boat *U-352* off the coast of North Carolina. This historic event resulted in the war's second U-boat sinking by US forces, the first US capture of enemy combatants, and a Navy Cross awarded to her commanding officer, Maurice Jester, from Chincoteague, Virginia. *Icarus* operated in the greater Hampton Roads area during World War II, including a rearmament in Norfolk. (Courtesy of the US Coast Guard.)

USCGC *Vigorous* arrived at its new homeport at Joint Expeditionary Base Little Creek–Fort Story, Virginia Beach, Friday, July 31, 2014. *Vigorous* was the first of two medium-endurance cutters from Cape May, New Jersey, to be relocated to Little Creek. The USCGC *Dependable* arrived in 2015. (Photograph by PO Walter Shinn, courtesy of the US Coast Guard.)

The crew of USCGC *Frank Drew* (WLM 557) worked with Navy sailors from Amphibious Construction Battalion 2, Beachmaster Unit 2, and Naval Beach Group 2 out of Joint Expeditionary Base Little Creek to remove two washed-ashore buoys from Chic's Beach and ocean-view areas of Virginia Beach and Norfolk in October 2013. The buoys washed ashore during storms that passed through Hampton Roads. (Photograph by PO David Weydert, courtesy of the US Coast Guard.)

A Coast Guard rescue crew from Station Portsmouth unloads passengers from the cruise ship *Spirit of Nantucket* after it ran aground in the Atlantic Intracoastal Waterway approximately eight miles north of the Virginia–North Carolina state line on Thursday, November 8, 2007. (Photograph by Kip Waldow, courtesy of the US Coast Guard.)

Navy Junior Reserve Officers' Training Corps members from Norview High School and US Naval Sea Cadet Corps members from the Hampton Roads area engage with Coast Guard members through the Cadet Mentorship Assistance Program's kick-off event held at US Coast Guard Base Portsmouth on May 17, 2021. Outreach like this is critical in helping the public understand the Coast Guard mission. It is also an effective recruiting tool. (Photograph by Kate Kilroy, courtesy of the US Coast Guard.)

USCGC *Flying Fish*, an 87-foot patrol boat homeported at JEB Little Creek in Virginia Beach, steams north alongside the Chesapeake Bay Bridge-Tunnel off Virginia Beach, February 15, 2018. The cutter's crew of 12 primarily conducts search and rescue and marine fisheries enforcement missions in the lower Chesapeake Bay and off Virginia's coast. (Photograph by PO Corinne Zilnicki, courtesy of the US Coast Guard.)

The first group of Coast Guard women assigned to sea duty pose for a photograph onboard the USCGC *Unimak* on May 9, 1973, in Yorktown. Shortly after this photograph was taken, the USCG Women's Reserve ended and became a full and equal part of the active-duty Coast Guard. (Courtesy of the US Coast Guard.)

The CGC *Cuyahoga* is pictured pier-side in the 1940s. She saw combat in World War II, but later sank in 1978 after colliding with a vessel in the Chesapeake Bay. Eleven personnel on the boat perished, with eighteen surviving by using the *Cuyahoga's* small Boston Whaler as a lifeboat. The remains of the ship were recovered and then sunk again as an artificial reef. (Courtesy of the US Coast Guard.)

A Coast Guard 25-foot response boat–small from Station Little Creek escorts the USS *Harry S. Truman* (CVN 75) through the southern branch of the Elizabeth River in Portsmouth in November 2014. The USCGC *Sea Horse* (WPB 87361), homeported in Portsmouth, and response boat crews from Station Portsmouth provided escort for the carrier during the transit. (Courtesy of the US Coast Guard.)

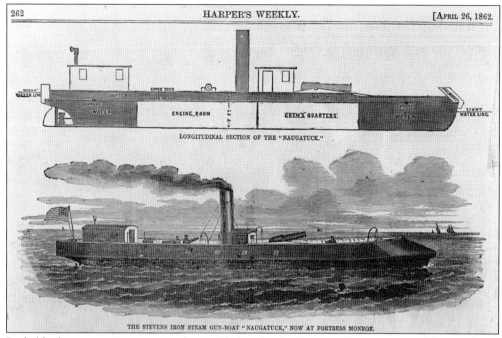

LONGITUDINAL SECTION OF THE "NAUGATUCK."

THE STEVENS IRON STEAM GUN-BOAT "NAUGATUCK," NOW AT FORTRESS MONROE.

Probably the most unique cutter to have sailed under the Revenue Service ensign, *Naugatuck* was a gun battery that could partially submerge for protection. She displaced 120 tons, was steam-driven, and mounted a 100-pounder Parrott rifle and two 12-pounders. She was originally built in 1844 and entered the Revenue Cutter Service in 1862, apparently as something of a gift by her builder who hoped to generate interest in his novel design. She took part in the famous battle between the CSS *Virginia* and USS *Monitor* in Hampton Roads and in the attack on Drewry's Bluff, Virginia, in 1862. She also served as a guard vessel in New York Harbor later in the war. She was removed from service in 1872. Here, she is depicted in a *Harper's Weekly* article from 1862. (Courtesy of the US Coast Guard.)

The USCGC *Spencer* (WMEC 905) pulls into the harbor behind the guided-missile frigate USS *Klakring* (FFG 42) while in Montevideo, Uruguay, for a port visit in 2010. Southern Seas is a US Southern Command–directed operation that provides US and international forces the opportunity to operate in a multinational environment. At the time of this photograph, *Spencer* was stationed in Boston. However, she shifted homeports to Portsmouth in 2021. (Photograph by PO Darryl Wood, courtesy of the US Navy.)

This is a World War II–era photograph of a Coast Guard fireboat. The Coast Guard relies on fireboats to put out fires at sea and, at times, on piers. Fireboats use seawater pumped from below the vessel to put out fires. (Courtesy of the US Coast Guard.)

Jessamine, built in 1881 and pictured here in 1886, was an example of a paddlewheel tender. The evolution of the lighthouse and buoy tender is directly related to the functions they served, the materials and technology available at the time of construction, and the mission and traditions of the administering agency. Over time, their consistent function has been to service aids to navigation, such as buoys, light stations, and lightships. As the technology and care of aids to navigation evolved and changed, so have the vessels that serviced them. In more recent years, tender duties have expanded to include search and rescue, icebreaking, military readiness, and law enforcement—reflecting the expanded mission of the modern US Coast Guard. (Courtesy of the National Archives.)

A rescue launch from the USCGC *Ingham* returns to the ship with a group of Cuban refugees who were stranded on a small coral island 14 miles off the coast of Cuba. These refugees were first sighted from a Coast Guard plane, whereupon a radio call through the Seventh Coast Guard District Search and Rescue Center in Miami, Florida, notified the *Ingham* of the distressed Cubans while the cutter was operating in the Florida Straits. The 327-foot cutter *Ingham* was based in Norfolk. (Courtesy of the US Coast Guard.)

The crew of the USCGC *Frank Drew* (WLM 557) worked with Navy sailors from Amphibious Construction Battalion 2, Beachmaster Unit 2, and Naval Beach Group 2 out of Joint Expeditionary Base Little Creek to remove two washed-ashore buoys from Chic's Beach and oceanview areas of Virginia Beach and Norfolk in October 2013. The buoys washed ashore during storms that passed through Hampton Roads. (Photograph by PO3 David Weydert, courtesy of the US Coast Guard.)

The US Coast Guard small harbor tug USCGC *Chock* (WYTL 65602) and a Coast Guard patrol craft escort the Soviet Sovremenny-class guided-missile destroyer *Otlichnny* as the ship departs from the roadstead following a five-day visit to Naval Station Norfolk in July 1989. (Photograph by PO Tracy Didas, courtesy of the US Coast Guard.)

This World War I–era artwork bears the inscription "E.P. Griffith, Newport News, Virginia." This ship was built in Newport News in 1908. She was temporarily under Navy control during World War I (1917), but maintained her Coast Guard crew. She reverted to the Coast Guard in 1919. (Courtesy of the US Coast Guard.)

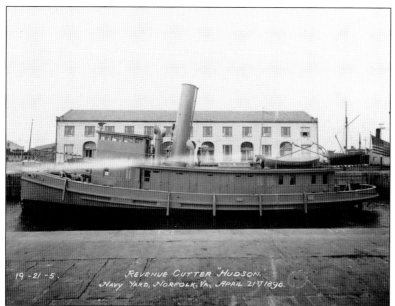

This is a press photo of the revenue cutter *Hudson* from 1898. She was stationed at the Norfolk Navy Yard, now known as Norfolk Naval Shipyard. Prior to 1917, all Navy and Coast Guard vessels were stationed at the Navy Yard. (Courtesy of the US Coast Guard.)

The USCGC *Point Bonita* (WPB 82347), homeported in Portsmouth, takes part in a hostile party demonstration put on by the Coast Guard for Missions Day attendees. The *Point Bonita* was one of the vessels that participated in Coast Guard Missions Day at Reserve Training Center Yorktown in 1999. (Photograph by PO Telfair Brown, courtesy of the US Coast Guard.)

The US Coast Guard took command of a Navy Cyclone-class patrol ship on March 5 at the Naval Amphibious Base in Little Creek, Virginia, for testing and evaluation. The USS *Thunderbolt* officially became the Coast Guard cutter *Thunderbolt* in March and was transferred back to the Navy on July 17, 1999. (Photograph by PO David Schuerholz, courtesy of the US Coast Guard.)

US Coast Guard members take a test ride aboard a new deployable pursuit boat in 1999. It was built to outrun or catch drug smugglers and is generally deployed from a larger ship. (Photograph by PO Dion Short, courtesy of the US Coast Guard.)

The USCGC *Campbell* shares a pier with USCGC *Eagle* at Little Creek Amphibious Base. The crew of the *Campbell* participated in three weeks of training and drills at the base. (Courtesy of the US Coast Guard.)

The Coast Guard patrol boat USCGC *Manticus* (WPB 1315) approaches the Soviet Slava-class guided-missile cruiser *Marshal Ustinov* (CG 088), which is being escorted into port by the cutter USCGC *Bear* (WMEC 901). *Marshal Ustinov* and two other Russian warships made the first-ever Soviet naval visit to a US military port in July 1989. (Courtesy of the US Coast Guard.)

This image shows the USCGC *Manning* at anchor in 1927. She was active in the Coast Guard from 1898 to 1930, participating in the Spanish American War and World War I as part of the US Navy. (Courtesy of the US Coast Guard.)

The USCGC *Manning* is shown here at Norfolk in December 1920. Several men are visible topside, perhaps waiting to go on liberty. A harbor tug is visible in the left foreground. (Courtesy of the US Coast Guard.)

The crew aboard the USCGC *Shearwater* (WPB 87349), an 87-foot patrol boat homeported in Portsmouth, leads the Parade of Ships navigating through the Elizabeth River on Wednesday, June 6, 2012. Naval ships participating in the parade included ships from the US Navy, US Coast Guard, National Oceanic and Atmospheric Administration, and US Army Corps of Engineers. (Photograph by PO Walter Shinn, courtesy of the US Coast Guard.)

This is an aerial starboard side view of the nuclear-powered aircraft carrier USS *Theodore Roosevelt* (CVN 71) tied up on the north side of pier No. 12 at the Norfolk Naval Base in 1996. A medium endurance US Coast Guard cutter is moored on the south side of the pier. (Courtesy of the US Coast Guard.)

This is an aerial starboard quarter view of the Coast Guard coastal buoy tender *Red Cedar* (WLM 688) underway. *Red Cedar* was awarded the Meritorious Unit Commendation for her salvage of the USCGC *Cuyahoga*. (Courtesy of the US Coast Guard.)

USRC *Harriet Lane* saw service with the US Revenue Cutter Service, US Navy, and the Confederate Navy. Some sources report that Harriet Lane (as a Union vessel) fired the first naval shot of the Civil War. She was only in service from 1857 to 1864, primarily out of Norfolk. Harriet Lane, niece of Pres. James Buchanan, is so important to the Coast Guard that she has another ship named after her, USCGC *Harriet Lane* (WMEC 903), based out of Portsmouth. (Courtesy of the US Coast Guard.)

The USCGC *Elm* and *Beluga* celebrate the Coast Guard's 221st birthday at the 2011 Coast Guard Day celebration in August 2011 in Portsmouth. The crews of CGC *Elm* and *Beluga* were available for tours during the celebration. (Courtesy of the US Coast Guard.)

This is a 1931 photograph of the USCGC *Carrabasset* (AT 35) in Norfolk. Originally launched as a tugboat in 1919, the ship was decommissioned in 1922 and transferred to the Treasury Department for use by the Coast Guard in 1924. (Courtesy of the Sargeant Memorial Collection, Norfolk Public Library).

This 1942 photograph shows two Coast Guard fireboats at Pinner's Point in Portsmouth. As the Coast Guard expanded its presence in the area, all vessels transitioned to Base Portsmouth and Little Creek. (Courtesy of the US Coast Guard.)

This 1942 photograph shows the Coast Guard fireboat *Agnes Sterling*. The ship was acquired by the War Shipping Administration during World War II and was returned to her owner in 1946. (Courtesy of the US Coast Guard.)

This early-20th-century photograph shows Patrol Boat 222, likely out for a family cruise. These patrol boats were previously called Inshore Patrol Cutters. The Coast Guard had several hundred of them built, and they were all unnamed. In 1933, she was transferred to the US Navy and operated as Yard Patrol Boat 22. (Courtesy of the Sargeant Memorial Collection, Norfolk Public Library.)

This is a 1930 photograph of the Coast Guard Lake-class cutter *Mendota* docked in Norfolk. Launched in 1928 and commissioned the next year, the ship was transferred to the British Royal Navy in 1941 and renamed the HMS *Culver*. During service in the Royal Navy, the ship was torpedoed by a German U-boat and sunk on January 31, 1942. (Courtesy of the Sargeant Memorial Collection, Norfolk Public Library.)

In this photograph from 2008, Coast Guard crews demonstrate the capabilities of a 45-foot fast response boat from Station Little Creek and a 24-foot special purpose craft—*Shallow Water* from Station Chincoteague in the Elizabeth River near Portsmouth. The boats provide Coast Guard crews with enhanced capabilities to fulfill their Homeland Security missions. (Photograph by PO Mark Jones, courtesy of the US Coast Guard.)

This is a 1937 photograph of the Treasury-class cutter *Bibb* (WPG-31) pier-side in Norfolk. Bibb was commissioned in 1937 and was active in World War II providing escort duty across the Atlantic, primarily to North Africa. During the Vietnam War, she assisted in the evacuation of John Kerry, later US secretary of state. She was decommissioned in 1985. (Courtesy of the Sargeant Memorial Collection, Norfolk Public Library.)

This is a 1923 photograph of the Coast Guard tugboat *Tioga* in Norfolk. Sources differ on the name of this boat. However, most agree that from 1894 to 1934, she was known as *Calumet* (WYT 86), a cutter/tug. (Courtesy of the Sargeant Memorial Collection, Norfolk Public Library.)

The USCGC *Daniel Tarr* (WPC 1136) is moored at Sector Field Office Galveston, Texas, during its commissioning ceremony on January 10, 2020. Vice Adm. Scott Buschman, Coast Guard Atlantic Area commander, presided over the ceremony. *Tarr* is named after Daniel Tarr, a hero of Guadalcanal in World War II and a resident of Chincoteague. Tarr piloted the first landing craft of the infamous amphibious landing. (Photograph by Sector Houston-Galveston Drone Team, courtesy of the US Coast Guard.)

The crew of the Coast Guard cutter *Bear* offloaded more than 1,851 pounds of cocaine, with a wholesale value of more than $22 million, at Coast Guard Base Miami Beach in November 2012. A Coast Guard law enforcement detachment onboard the HNLMS *Van Amstel* (Royal Netherlands Navy), assisted in recovering 42 bales of cocaine during a counter-drug patrol in the Caribbean. (Photograph by PO3 Sabrina Elgammal, courtesy of the US Coast Guard.)

The USCGC *Ingham* (WHEC 35) was commissioned in 1936 and decommissioned after 52 years of faithful service in 1988. *Ingham* served with distinction in the Vietnam War, earning a still-unsurpassed two Presidential Unit Citations. She is pictured here in Norfolk, but she is now a floating museum in Key West. (Courtesy of the US Coast Guard.)

The USCG *Sledge* (WLR 75303) pushes a floating Coast Guard building down the Elizabeth River in Norfolk. Research did not determine the use of this facility, but it was likely a mobile command post, residence, or office. (Courtesy of the US Coast Guard.)

The USCGC *Sledge* (WLR 75303) is pictured here in 1956. She is a construction tender and is one of eight in the Coast Guard. Her role is to perform maintenance on essential aids to navigation, keeping the seas safe for navigation. (Courtesy of the US Coast Guard.)

The *Narcissus* (WAGL 38) was built for the Coast Guard in 1939. She transferred to the US Navy along with the Coast Guard in 1941. Her primary duties involved maintaining aids to navigation. She operated out of Portsmouth from 1940 until 1971, when she was sold to Guyana. This photograph is from 1956. (Courtesy of the Portsmouth Public Library Special Collections.)

USCGC *Marion* (WSC 145) was a patrol boat in service to the Coast Guard from 1927 to 1962. This 1956 photograph shows her on the Elizabeth River. She conducted several missions in World War II, but is most known for the oceanographic work she did for the Coast Guard. The great crane at the Norfolk Naval Shipyard can be seen in the background. (Courtesy of the Portsmouth Public Library Special Collections.)

USCGC *Gallatin* (WHEC 721) was a Treasury-class cutter that served the US Coast Guard from 1968 to 2014. She was stationed in Charleston, South Carolina, but is seen here on the Elizabeth River near Norfolk Naval Shipyard. The photograph is undated but is most likely from the 1970s. (Courtesy of the Portsmouth Public Library Special Collections.)

USCGC *Dependable* (WMEC 626), a 210-foot medium endurance cutter, works with the Dominican Republic naval vessel *Aldebaran* in August 2015 to transfer two people who were discovered lost at sea on their 20-foot vessel. Dependable returned to Joint Expeditionary Base Little Creek–Fort Story in August of that year following a successful drug interdiction of 650 pounds of marijuana, halting drug smugglers off the coast of Jamaica, migrant repatriation, and search and rescue. (Photograph by Ens. Andrea Davis, courtesy of the US Coast Guard.)

USCGC *Vigorous* (WMEC 626), a 210-foot medium endurance cutter, is moored in Portsmouth after participating in the Parade of Ships, June 6, 2012. The Parade of Ships hosts assets from international fleets along with the US Navy, Coast Guard, and other agencies. *Vigorous* is based out of Joint Expeditionary Base Little Creek–Fort Story. (Photograph by Smn. Andrea Davis, courtesy of the US Coast Guard.)

Three

ACTION

The crew of the USCGC *Hornbeam* (WLB 394) secures the buoy chain after pulling a buoy out of the water as part of the Joint Civilian Orientation Conference (JCOC) demonstration at Reserve Training Center Yorktown. The JCOC, sponsored each year by the secretary of defense, brings together 60 noted civilians from around the country—a broad cross-section of opinion leaders—and gives them a weeklong, intense orientation on the US military. The program begins with high-level briefings at the Pentagon and then takes the participants to various installations across the country for hands-on experiences. (Photograph by PO Telfair Brown, courtesy of the US Coast Guard.)

The USCGC *Seneca* was built by Newport News Shipbuilding and delivered to the Coast Guard (then Revenue Cutter Service) in 1908. Her mission was to find and destroy derelict ships that were hazards to navigation. This explains the large gun being inspected by the crew and a couple of officers. During World War I, she was one of five cutters that the Navy took to the war in Europe. Interestingly, she was on location at Gibraltar on November 11, 1918, when the armistice was signed that ended the war. (Courtesy of the Library of Congress.)

Sailors assigned to the USCGC *Legare* (WMEC 912) conduct small-boat training in a 25-foot over-the-horizon boat. *Legare*, homeported in Portsmouth, conducted a three-month patrol across the Atlantic Ocean in 2009. The ship visited several countries in west and central Africa supporting Africa Partnership Station. (Photograph by PO Thomas M. Blue, courtesy of the US Coast Guard.)

A Coast Guard Maritime Security Response Team (MSRT) member provides cover during a helicopter fast-rope boarding May 4, 2015, aboard the civilian passenger ship the *Spirit of Norfolk* during an MSRT training demonstration in the Chesapeake Bay near Naval Station Norfolk. The MSRT is a specialized response team with advanced counter-terrorism skills and tactics. (Courtesy of the US Coast Guard.)

Five active-duty members stand for a photograph at the former Coast Guard station in Virginia Beach holding the Coast Guard flag on May 24, 2013, after running 34 miles to raise awareness for fallen shipmates. Despite a continuous downpour, the final event took place at Base Portsmouth with about 80 participants, including a few enjoying the view in strollers. (Photograph by Ens. Duane Zitta, courtesy of the US Coast Guard.)

Fireman Collin Kennedy heaves around a mooring line aboard USCGC *Hamilton* (WMSL 753) after pulling into port in Naples, Italy, on April 20, 2021. *Hamilton* was on a routine deployment in the US Sixth Fleet area of operations in support of US national interests and security in Europe and Africa. Naples has long been a popular place for ships of both the Navy and Coast Guard to visit for liberty and maintenance. US Sixth Fleet is headquartered in Naples, and its primary responsibility includes the entire Mediterranean Sea. (Photograph by PO Sydney Phoenix, courtesy of the US Coast Guard.)

This 1999 photograph shows the crew of the USCGC *Elm* (WLB 204) demonstrating the procedures for pulling a buoy out of the water for maintenance. The *Elm* was one of the vessels that participated in Coast Guard Missions Day at Reserve Training Center Yorktown. (Photograph by PO Telfair Brown, courtesy of the US Coast Guard.)

Coast Guard Station Portsmouth tows the sailing vessel *Evonne* in August 2015. Crews from the USCGC *Heron* and Station Portsmouth worked together to dewater the sailing vessel and tow it to Blue Water Marina, Portsmouth. (Courtesy of the US Coast Guard.)

This is an aerial view of Base Portsmouth under construction in the early 1970s. A large cutter is visible in the foreground. The completed base would have an additional pier and multiple support buildings. The Coast Guard also constructed a seawall along the edge of the property, to the right of the cutter. (Courtesy of the US Coast Guard.)

This is a 1960s photograph of Base Norfolk (Berkeley Station). Two large cutters, one small cutter, and a tug are visible. The land and piers seen here are now under private management, operating as a shipyard that primarily serves the Navy and Coast Guard. (Courtesy of the US Coast Guard.)

This early-1970s photograph shows a Coast Guard helicopter conducting operations off the coast of Virginia. A Sikorski HH52 Seaguard, this single-engine, amphibious, all-weather helicopter was placed into service in 1961. The aircraft extended the range the Coast Guard could conduct search and rescue operations. The Coast Guard purchased 175 of the aircraft, which operated in all Coast Guard areas of responsibility. They are no longer in service. (Courtesy of the US Coast Guard.)

The USCGC *Conifer* (WLB 301) was a buoy tender that was in service from 1943 until 2000. She operated out of Portsmouth and Morehead City, North Carolina. During World War II, she was part of the US Navy as part of Task Force 24, whose primary responsibility was anti-submarine patrols in the North Atlantic. After decommissioning, *Conifer* became known as the MV *Hope*, responding to those in need after natural disasters as a part of Friend Ships. (Courtesy of the US Coast Guard.)

This 1960s photograph shows the Grumman HU-16 amphibian seaplane. This aircraft was known as an "Albatross" or "Goat." They were operated by the Coast Guard from 1951 to 1983. They were used for a variety of missions, including search and rescue. Even though they were capable of water landings to conduct rescue operations, they rarely did so. (Courtesy of the US Coast Guard.)

A Coast Guard maritime and security safety crew, temporarily deployed from San Francisco, provides an escort for the USS *Cole* (DDG 67) as she returns to Norfolk Naval Shipyard on the Elizabeth River. The Coast Guard was providing escorts for Navy ships returning to Norfolk and Virginia Beach after Hurricane Irene passed through the area in August 2011. (Photograph by PO David Weydert, courtesy of the US Coast Guard.)

Coast Guard cutters fight a fire on the pier at Pinner's Point in Portsmouth. The fire, which broke out in May 1964, lasted for three days. While the Coast Guard's primary mission is on the water, it is not unheard of for dangers to arise onshore despite strict safety regulations. The fire ended up destroying two piers and damaging several moored vessels. (Courtesy of the US Coast Guard.)

In the aftermath of the hurricane that swept the Atlantic coast on September 14, 1944, thirteen crew members of a ship that foundered off the Virginia coast were brought to safety by means of a breeches buoy by Coast Guard crewmen from the Virginia Lifeboat Station at the Virginia Beach waterfront. Rescue operations were begun while the storm was at its height and the ship was in danger of breaking up on the beach. The lifesaving service used the breeches buoy technique because it was common for ships to founder near the coast. It requires shore personnel to shoot a line from the shore to the ship. Then, the persons in distress are attached to the line and pulled to the shore by men on the beach. (Courtesy of the Library of Congress).

This photograph shows an experimental air cushion vessel being tested by the Coast Guard in late 1971. The vessel could operate on the water and on land. It was evaluated for about eight months, but it was not procured by the Coast Guard as it was determined that newer technology would benefit the service better. Norfolk Naval Shipyard is in the background, along with its great crane. (Courtesy of the Portsmouth Public Library Special Collections.)

This early-20th-century photograph shows the Portsmouth Buoy Depot. Most of the buoys were organized on a large wood pier like this one, ready to be lifted onto barges (like the one at left) or ships. Several depot employees are also visible. (Courtesy of the US Coast Guard.)

This 1950s photograph shows the access gate for Berkeley Station, the home of most Coast Guard vessels, especially cutters, prior to the opening of Base Portsmouth. Access to the base was controlled by an armed sentry. (Courtesy of the US Coast Guard.)

This early-20th-century photograph shows buoys on a pier and a Coast Guard tug. The bottom of each buoy is rigged with chains to help it stay in position in the water. The large chains take up most of the foreground. Buoy parts are also visible, as are an additional boat in the right background. (Courtesy of the US Coast Guard.)

Pictured in the early 20th century is one of many buoy piers in Portsmouth. A sidewheel steamer is also visible in a slip on the right. These piers would have been on the opposite side of the Elizabeth River from Berkeley Station.

An armed Coast Guard sentry is on alert, guarding pier access at Berkeley Station in Norfolk. The photograph is likely from the late 1940s or early 1950s. In the event of inclement weather, the sentry could monitor his post from the guardhouse behind him. (Courtesy of the US Coast Guard.)

This is the sign that visitors encountered at Base Portsmouth in the 1960s when it was downtown. Buoys and a barge are visible in the background behind the sign. The men admiring the sign are unidentified. (Courtesy of the US Coast Guard.)

The Coast Guard piers at the Randolph Street slip in downtown Portsmouth are pictured in 1928. The tug *Laurel* is in the left foreground and a larger unidentified tug is in the background. The larger tug is stopping at the quay wall to pick up buoys at the yard. *Laurel* might be at the pier to pick up some coal for her engines from the barge next to her. (Courtesy of the US Coast Guard.)

This early-20th-century photograph shows the buoy yard in Portsmouth. Two children are in the image. Additionally, quite a few concrete weights are visible. These weights would be attached to the chains that hold the buoys in place at sea. It is possible that each man in the photograph is standing next to their area of responsibility. (Courtesy of the US Coast Guard.)

This is a busy Coast Guard metal fabrication production building at the buoy depot in Portsmouth in the 1940s. The machines on the right are metal lathes. The left side of the image includes drill presses, saws, a large lathe, and other machinery. (Courtesy of the US Coast Guard.)

These 1940s photographs show the top and bottom of a large, lighted buoy being transported by tractor at Berkeley Station in Norfolk or at the Navy Yard in Portsmouth. The tractor is from the Navy Yard. (Both, courtesy of the US Coast Guard.)

This 1925 photograph shows the keeper's dwelling at Portsmouth. Operational lighthouses, before automation, required round-the-clock care and support. To ease the burden on the lighthouse keepers, dwellings like these were constructed. (Courtesy of the US Coast Guard.)

The Base Portsmouth commanding officer receives an award in front of his men in the 1950s. A cutter mast and the Base Portsmouth sign are in the background. None of the personnel are identified. (Courtesy of the US Coast Guard.)

This is the paint storehouse at Base Portsmouth in 1925. Because of the flammable nature of paint and its associated thinners, strict safety precautions were taken. Several 1920s vehicles and concrete buoy blocks are also visible. (Courtesy of the US Coast Guard.)

This mid-20th-century photograph shows the local Coast Guard softball team taking a moment for a team photograph before a game. The coach is at center. (Courtesy of the US Coast Guard.)

This is a fantastic aerial view of the Portsmouth Buoy Depot from the 1940s. The lightship *Winter Quarter* is on the left. Buoys await deployment on the piers. Several large and small Coast Guard vessels are also visible. (Courtesy of the US Coast Guard.)

This aerial view of the buoy depot in Portsmouth is from the late 1950s or early 1960s. An unidentified lightship and several large and small Coast Guard vessels are present. (Courtesy of the US Coast Guard.)

In another aerial view of the buoy depot in Portsmouth from the late 1950s or early 1960s, the lightship *Chesapeake* is in port as well as several Coast Guard vessels, including a buoy barge. (Courtesy of the US Coast Guard.)

Two large cutters, possibly buoy tenders, are visible at the buoy depot in Portsmouth. Additionally, several small cutters and boats are visible in the slip at center. (Courtesy of the US Coast Guard.)

The buoy depot in Portsmouth is seen here in the 1960s. The lightship *Relief* is at lower left. Quite a few large and small cutters are also present. (Courtesy of the US Coast Guard.)

The lightship *Relief* is seen here in more detail. Of note is the quantity of lifeboats on the pier. Boats like these would have been used by the lifesaving service to rescue mariners and swimmers in peril. The Coast Guard used them long after the two services merged. (Courtesy of the US Coast Guard.)

A Coast Guard forklift driver receives an award from a Coast Guard officer at Berkeley Station in Norfolk. The photograph is not dated, but it is likely from the 1950s, given the style of the forklift. (Courtesy of the US Coast Guard.)

This is a Coast Guard floatplane from the 1920s. Even in the early part of the 20th century when aviation was at its beginning, the Coast Guard used aircraft to aid in search and rescue. (Courtesy of the US Coast Guard.)

A Sikorski HH52A Seaguard amphibious single-engine helicopter sits on the tarmac in Elizabeth City, North Carolina, in the 1970s. These helicopters, critical in search and rescue operations, served in the Hampton Roads area for decades beginning in the 1960s. (Courtesy of the US Coast Guard.)

A Coast Guard fireboat provides a capability demonstration on the Elizabeth River in the 1950s. (Courtesy of the US Coast Guard.)

Eight men pose in front of the Coast Guard fireboat station in Norfolk. A Coast Guard sentry is visible on the right. The date is unknown, but it can be assumed based on the vehicles in the background that it is sometime in the 1950s. (Courtesy of the US Coast Guard.)

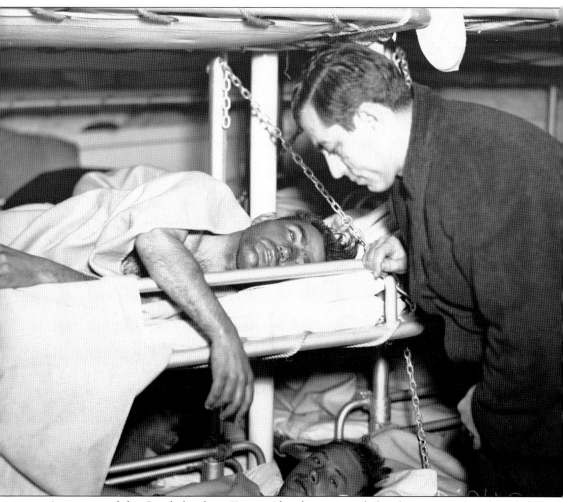

A survivor of the Greek freighter *Tzenny Chandris* is attended to by personnel on board the USCGC *Mendota* in 1937. The *Chandris* was lost at sea for two days off the coast of North Carolina. They were rescued by the *Mendota*. (Courtesy of the Sargeant Memorial Collection, Norfolk Public Library.)

Cutters from throughout the Fifth Coast Guard District are gathered at Coast Guard Base Portsmouth to participate in a cutter roundup Tuesday, August 22, 2017. The cutter roundup provides joint training opportunities for the crews. (Photograph by auxiliarist Trey Clifton, courtesy of the US Coast Guard.)

The Coast Guard cutter *Eagle* is shown here moored up at the High Street Landing in downtown Portsmouth on Friday, September 13, 2013. The *Eagle* makes frequent visits to Portsmouth, and is usually available for tours during visits. (Photograph by PO David Weydert, courtesy of the US Coast Guard.)

This 1907 postcard shows a lifesaving drill at Cape Henry Life Station. The card was part of a set published by a firm in Norfolk for the 1907 Jamestown Exposition, which celebrated 300 years since the founding of the colony. This card could be mailed to any location in the United States, Canada, Mexico, or Cuba for 1¢. (Courtesy of the US Coast Guard.)

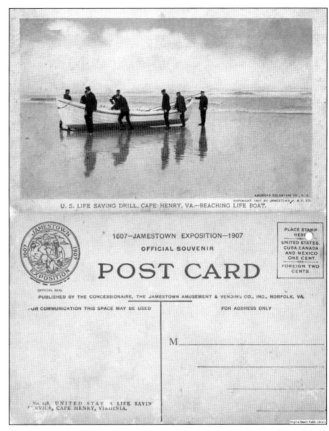

Ens. Matt Alex, stationed aboard the USCGC *Northland* (WMEC 904), inspects a fishing net while conducting a fishery boarding off the coast of New Jersey in 2006. The crew of the *Northland* stood a two-month living marine resources patrol to ensure all fishing vessels in the region were operating safely and legally. (Photograph by PO Christopher Evanson, courtesy of the US Coast Guard.)

Crew members from the US Coast Guard cutter *Rollin Fritch* and partners from the Department of Defense look on from the cutter's small boat as PO1 Brian Johnson, an aviation survival technician from Air Station Elizabeth City, descends into the water to retrieve two Air Force pilots during a joint-service search and rescue exercise on October 22, 2020, near Virginia Beach. The exercise was a joint operation among the Coast Guard, Air Force, and Navy to ensure successful coordination in the event of a large-scale search and rescue operation. (Photograph by Capt. Timothy Eason, courtesy of the US Coast Guard.)

First Lieutenant Aaron Johnson, a US Air Force pilot from Seymour Johnson Air Force Base, jumps into the water at the start of the joint-service search and rescue exercise on October 22, 2020, near Virginia Beach. (Photograph by PO3 Emily Velez, courtesy of the US Coast Guard.)

Coast Guard petty officer second class Rene Pena, damage controlman aboard Coast Guard cutter *Frank Drew* in Portsmouth, performs maintenance on a Bauer compressor on the ship on July 7, 2020. Pena is one of the crew members who work to maintain the *Frank Drew's* readiness. (Photograph by PO2 Katie Lipe, courtesy of the US Coast Guard.)

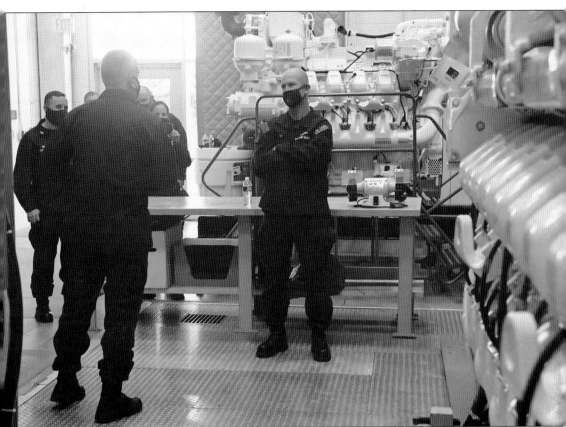

Vice Adm. Charles W. Ray, vice commandant of the US Coast Guard, and MCPO Charles R. Bushey, command master chief petty officer of the Coast Guard, visit Coast Guard Training Center Yorktown in March 2021. During the visit, they discussed issues concerning new ships and the rates available on them, new uniforms and their availability, and new technology that would continue to help the Coast Guard to remain ready, relevant, and responsive. (Photograph by PO2 Edward Wargo, courtesy of the US Coast Guard.)

Joint Civilian Orientation Conference participants and staff pose with an MH-60 crew from Air Station Elizabeth City after demonstrating the USCG search and rescue mission at US Coast Guard Base Portsmouth on November 8, 2019. Established in 1948, the Joint Civilian Orientation Conference is the Department of Defense's oldest and most prestigious public liaison program and is the only secretary of defense–sponsored outreach program that enables American business and community leaders to have a fully immersive experience with the military. (Photograph by auxiliarist Andy Winz, courtesy of the US Coast Guard.)

This 1930s photograph shows a horse and eight men pushing and pulling a rescue boat from the beach to the water in Virginia Beach. The ninth man rides the boat and guides the horse to where they want to deploy the boat. (Courtesy of the US Coast Guard.)

FIRST NEW GROUP OF SPARS TO RECEIVE BASIC MILITARY TRAINING IN 25 YEARS

This photographs shows the first new group of SPARS (US Coast Guard Women's Reserve) to receive military training since World War II. The Coast Guard Reserve Training Center in Yorktown hosted the training. (Courtesy of the US Coast Guard.)

In 1942, the Coast Guard ship *Icarus* (WPC 110) sank the German submarine *U-352* off the coast of North Carolina. She is shown here along with part of her crew and a group of armed US Marines in Charleston with 33 German prisoners from the *352*. The total crew complement of this class of submarine would have been around 45. After the war, *Icarus* was transferred back to the Coast Guard. She was refit and rearmed in Norfolk. (Courtesy of the National Archives)

An enlisted Coast Guard member and his horse stand the watch along the beach in Virginia Beach. The Coast Guard's mounted beach patrol provided critical security to the country's vulnerable coasts during World War II. (Courtesy of the US Coast Guard.)

An enlisted Coast Guard member and his dog stand the watch along the beach in Virginia Beach. The Coast Guard was responsible for protecting the shores from potential German invaders, especially from small craft that could easily escape detection from larger ships. Duty involved patrolling the beach on foot or horseback. (Courtesy of the US Coast Guard.)

This July 1861 page from *Harper's Weekly* celebrates the Fourth of July at Fort Monroe in Virginia. The panels include fireworks at the New York Fifth Regiment, the Second New York Infantry Regiment (also known as the Troy Regiment), illumination from the New York "Turner Rifles," and the Virginia Coast Guard firing salutes. On the date of publication, the United States had been at war with the Confederacy for less than three months. (Courtesy of the Library of Congress.)

A US Coast Guard Grumman E-2C Hawkeye (USCG serial 3501) is seen here on the tarmac at Naval Air Station Norfolk. In 1987, The USCG acquired eight E-2Cs, which were assigned to the newly commissioned CG Airborne Warning Squadron 1 based initially out of Norfolk. They were later transferred to a new facility at St. Augustine, Florida. (Courtesy of the US Coast Guard.)

73:—OCEAN FRONT AND PROMENADE LOOKING NORTH FROM COAST GUARD STATION.

VIRGINIA BEACH. VA.   44367

This 1951 linen postcard looks north from the US Coast Guard Station at Atlantic Avenue. As the card states, the oceanfront, boardwalk, and beach are visible, as well as hundreds of visitors. In the past 70 years, the view from the station has changed quite a bit, primarily with the addition of several multi-level hotels and condos. (Courtesy of the Mariners Museum.)

This 1934 photograph shows the Coast Guard headquarters staff, field commissioners, and an executive with the Norfolk Council of the Boy Scouts of America. They were about to take a cruise around the Chesapeake Bay onboard the USCGC *Travis* (WSC 153). The cruise was intended to be a conference on sea scouting. (Courtesy of the US Coast Guard.)

46244

This 1951 linen postcard shows a busy Virginia Beach boardwalk and the American flag flying high above the Coast Guard Station at Atlantic Avenue. The station is a Virginia Bach landmark and now operates as the Virginia Beach Surf and Rescue Museum. (Courtesy of the Mariners Museum.)

An MH-65 Dolphin helicopter rests on the deck of the Coast Guard cutter *Harriet Lane* in February 2021 during their 71-day patrol. *Harriet Lane* is homeported in Portsmouth. (Courtesy of the US Coast Guard.)

Navy and Coast Guard reservists participate in a fire fighting exercise at the Fleet Training Center. Every Coast Guard member stationed aboard a vessel goes through firefighting training. Due to the unique nature of ships, the ability to put out a fire quickly, or at least contain it, is critical. (Courtesy of the US Coast Guard.)

This postcard from the early 20th century shows a Coast Guard lifeboat being transported to the water by a group of people. It is unclear why women and children are in the picture, but it certainly makes the postcard more enjoyable. The Coast Guard presence in the area was a big tourist draw, and it was advertised extensively on postcards, such as this one. (Courtesy of the Virginia Beach Public Library.)

This c. 1945 photograph shows the street side view of the US Coast Guard Station at Atlantic Avenue. The flagpole is visible on the far right. (Courtesy of the Mariners Museum.)

These three tall houses, located behind a high brick wall on the edge of the Norfolk Naval Shipyard, were erected between 1837 and 1842 to serve as residences of the shipyard's commanding officers. Many of their details, mostly in a Greek Revival idiom, follow designs illustrated in the architectural pattern books of Asher Benjamin. The three houses survived the 1861 burning of the shipyard by evacuating Union forces and a burning the next year by departing Confederates. They are maintained by the Navy and still house the shipyard's ranking officers, with Quarters A, the largest of the three, traditionally serving as the commandant's house. Quarters B is the residence of the Coast Guard Atlantic Area commander. (Courtesy of the US Coast Guard.)

This late-19th-century photograph shows a Coast Guard man and his pet seagull. Not much is known about the photograph other than it was taken in Norfolk. (Courtesy of the US Coast Guard.)

The crew of the Coast Guard cutter *Legare* proudly stands on their flight deck next to nearly $400 million in seized cocaine and marijuana at Port Everglades, Florida, in April 2018. The drugs were interdicted off the coasts of Mexico and Central and South America by multiple Coast Guard cutters and Canadian naval vessels. The Coast Guard routinely interdicts shipments of this size bound for the United States. The *Legare* is one of six 270-foot cutters stationed in Portsmouth. (Photograph by Petty Officer Brandon Murray, courtesy of the US Coast Guard.)

The Coast Guard used beach patrols as early as 1871 (as part of the lifesaving service). Threats to American security on the shores rose significantly in the 1930s and 1940s. Here, the mounted patrol searches for suspicious ships and people who might do harm. (Courtesy of the Library of Congress.)

This photograph shows an experimental air cushion vessel being tested by the Coast Guard in late 1971. The vessel could operate on the water and on land. It was evaluated for about eight months, but it was not procured by the Coast Guard, as it was determined newer technology would benefit the service better. (Courtesy of the Portsmouth Public Library Special Collections.)

An experimental hovercraft air cushion vessel is shown being tested by the Coast Guard. This was one of three vessels acquired from the Navy after they returned from service in Vietnam. In the end, the Coast Guard determined that while these vessels provided a service, they could not replace traditional Coast Guard boats, ships, and aircraft. (Courtesy of the US Coast Guard.)

This 1971 photograph shows a Coast Guard vessel known as a "glass capsule." Its purpose could not be determined, but it was likely something under research and development during the Coast Guard's prolific R&D phase of the late 1960s and early 1970s. The vessel was self-propelled, but it had to be lowered into the water via crane. (Courtesy of the US Coast Guard.)

Discover Thousands of Local History Books
Featuring Millions of Vintage Images

Arcadia Publishing, the leading local history publisher in the United States, is committed to making history accessible and meaningful through publishing books that celebrate and preserve the heritage of America's people and places.

Find more books like this at
www.arcadiapublishing.com

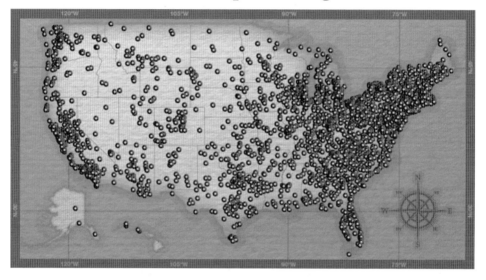

Search for your hometown history, your old stomping grounds, and even your favorite sports team.

Consistent with our mission to preserve history on a local level, this book was printed in South Carolina on American-made paper and manufactured entirely in the United States. Products carrying the accredited Forest Stewardship Council (FSC) label are printed on 100 percent FSC-certified paper.

MADE IN THE